The Art of Being a Bitch

THE ART OF BEING A BITCH

BY K.C. MENDOZA

I dedicate this book to all the
great Bitches and Pentches out there
finding the key to their own
Bitch-Dom.

TABLE OF CONTENTS

STOP! READ THIS FIRST!

After self-publishing my FIRST book, I discovered all the GODDAMN MISTAKES IT HAS, and I also received confused and divided questions. So let me address them here.

THE GENDER THING

When my book gets picked up, the first question I get is, "Is this book for women only?"

NO.

This book is for anyone who wants advice, read stories, and laugh. Of course, as it seems, my writing contains many "Bitch" and "Girl," BUT if you can read past that, the message it has is UNISEXUAL, UNISEX, Uni... whatever. You get my point.

THE AGE THING

When I did a pre-order special, I got messages asking me if this book was for kids under 13. Now, I am SURE some parents will want to hide my lousy mouth from the precious ears of their offspring. BUT I AM SURE your kids have access to YOUTUBE and dude……….

YouTube is riddled with bad words, all spectrums of gore words, sexual words, bad words, fucked up words, and made-up words that my 37-year-old ass doesn't understand. So, if you can look past my lousy mouth, I believe my message is clear and ultimately sweet.

THE CREDIBILITY THING

This is probably the MAIN question I get from people.

WHO NEEDS TO READ A BOOK ABOUT BEING A BITCH?

So, as I tried explaining this repeatedly, this book isn't to teach you how to be a mean, disrespectful, sad, fake bitch, etc. All those bad bitch connotations are out the window. No.

There isn't a master's degree in Bitch-DOM, but from one bitch to another, I feel this book is to ultimately unite with badass Bitches and create a community of self-respect, respect for others, and badassery.

THE MISTAKES THING

For all who purchased my FIRST EDITION: I am not only in debt to you and in LOVE with you, but I also apologize for the many mistakes it has. Remember, I didn't say I was PERFECT. I am just a good Bitch who is grateful.

But I do love that you bought my book without it EVEN CONTAINING A TABLE OF CONTENTS! THANK YOU, THANK YOU, AND THANK YOU!

Seriously, sometimes, I look at my FIRST EDITION, and I am in tears that many of you purchased my book with mistakes. But that's why this fat-ass loves you to the moon's anus and back. As for those purchasing this EDITION, I will apologize in advance for the new mistakes it might have.

THE WRITING THING

I also received questions about future books. So this is where I am going to drop some titles on you in the future. I am writing more books ranging from self-help to fiction.
 In life, I have always thought I wanted to be an actress, a teacher, a singer, or a musician. I am not a singer, though I love throwing up some rhymes. I am not a musician, though I've banged some drums in my life.
But I am a writer and will continue that because writing makes me happy.

I AM A WRITER.

As for future titles, I have a short storybook filled with dark poems and stories. In addition, I have The Art of Being a Spiritual Bitch coming out. I am also in the process of getting my first novel published, so stay tuned, stay connected, and stay thirsty, my friends.

Thank you from the bottom of my wrinkly anus to the top of my lovely crown.

Introduction

If it weren't for my former best friend who angrily called
me a Bitch, I would have remained a dumb Bitch
throughout my teenage and early adult years.

What is a Dumb Bitch? A **Dumb Bitch** is someone who
acts tough but does nothing for themselves and everything
for others.

I, my friends, had been a Dumb Bitch for several years. I
was used to being treated like trash by peers and former
"friends," and this did not land well. I decided to sit with
my high school boyfriend one day instead of my friend, and
in disgust, she looked at me with demonic eyes. I swear a

laser shot out of her eyes and into my core. That laser shattered our friendship in seconds.

Not knowing what I had done, she felt betrayed and angry that I, for once, didn't listen to her every word. But during that moment, I didn't care. It didn't matter. I was tired of her, tired of the people who consistently made me feel less than what I was. I was tired of being tied to a one-sided friendship. Finally, I was able to rip myself from that. She hissed (I swear she did,) and she said,

"You're such a Bitch!"

This wasn't the typical "Hey Bitch!" we get when we happily see someone we haven't seen in a few weeks. Instead, this was an angry "Bitch!" and we didn't call each other that at any time during our friendship so, she meant it. And as she said it, her energy spewed from her mouth and into my energy vortex. I swear my aura picked up a few new colors embedded with shit stains, and well, I took it. I sat there, dumb and numbly smiling at my boyfriend, but I took her hatred. I soaked in it throughout the bus ride home.

What the fuck!?
Why did she call me a Bitch!
I am no Bitch!
I am a nice stupid girl who listens to everyone and everything! I am a person who tries to please everyone and never says no! I am a misunderstood angel amid high school drama! I never said anything to upset them! I stood quiet! And now, I'm a Bitch?!

As I stepped off the bus and into my boyfriend's house, my day was ruined. But I began to think about it.
Wait, I was a Bitch.

Not the kind of Bitch that people want to run over with the car, no. A good Bitch. A badass Bitch that takes shit from no one.

But I was a puppet looking for another master to pick up the wooden cross to which I was tied to. But not that day. I stood up to them.

Most importantly, I did something for myself. I finally voiced somewhat of a demand for where I wanted to be and what I wanted to do for myself. Finally, my puppet strings untied, and I felt my ass sit on the chair without it being held against me.

"I am a real boy!" said Pinocchio. And I was! It felt great to decide for myself. And I was going to try my best to continue. But this was all said and not done. It took me years of trials and tribulations, backstabs, slaps to the face, rides through hell and back to finally understand what my friend Liz now calls: *The Art of Being a Bitch*

Chapter 1: Your Inner Bitch

Being called a Bitch has positive and negative connotations. As for this book, I want you to focus on *the Good Bitch, the Boss-Bitch, the I-will-do-what-it-takes Bitch, and the Don't-you-Dare-Disrespect Bitch.* If you're looking for how to be a *Lazy Bitch, Whiney Bitch, or a plain-old-mean Bitch,* then this book is not for you.

Because finding your inner Bitch is tough! It will make you uncomfortable.

And sometimes, we will lose people in the process. Because once you begin to Bitch-up, you distance yourself from people who don't care or are used to mistreating you. And it hurts because separation sucks!

I considered myself to have many friends. But these people weren't my friends. So when I began to Bitch-up, I yanked out bad people like weeds inside a beautiful garden. These "friends" were stripping my roses and ripping my roots to shreds.

Since elementary school, I was in crowds of people, but I felt like the loneliest girl. This was a constant feeling throughout my childhood. And once I began to Bitch-up, I purchased a lawnmower that sucked in people as well.

My class was divided into two groups: The cool and uncool crowd. But unlike the losers' club, we weren't all that close. When one of us would fight, we would be thrown from one group to another to avoid being a loner in the outfield, which was worse. I spent many days shutting up because it was better to be in one of those groups than none at all.

When I would fight with one of them, the other one would call and pick me up. Of course, they did that with everyone. Each day, one of us was a basketball bouncing in their court. I didn't even know the reason behind their switching game; I guess I was never inside a group long enough to find out, but for the six hours of school time, we loved it. We really did!

I was "In" even when I wasn't.

There was one girl (let's call her Jan for the sake of not being sued). Not that I am going to be sued by someone that I went to elementary with, but we live in a "You-hurt-my-reputation-I'll-sue-you" kind of world. So, Jan sounds good.

Jan was the It girl. She was the Regina George of my elementary. Who is Regina George? For those of you who aren't Mean Girls fans, she was the main Bitch in that movie. Everyone hated her but couldn't look or get away. We knew she was it, and boy, was she a Bitch.

Nope. You guessed it. Not the good Bitch, either. She was the type of Bitch that this book isn't for. I'm sure she changed throughout the years, but she was the one who planted the seed to my retaliation years later.

The fact is: mean girls or no mean girls, I never really had the chance to stand up to her. My big sisters once chased her home because she had stolen something from me, and I was still afraid of her; even if my sisters had an army behind them, I would never speak up to her.

To be fair, I wasn't her only target. She would lock other people in the bathroom, shut the lights off, blame her friends for things she did, and get many of us in trouble just to get a laugh. Yes, even her friends. Her devoted followers. Exactly like Regina George.

Now, if you didn't get a chance to watch Mean Girls yet, there is a part towards the end of the movie (yes, spoiler alert!) where Regina George gets hit by a bus (but survives), and I sometimes wondered what would have happened if Jan was hit by a bus as well.

Of course, I am kidding. I think.

Yes, I describe elementary school years, but remember, this prompted my inner Bitch to yell out years later. Having friends take advantage of me caused me trouble years later. I was fed up with this that at one point, I stabbed one of my "friends" with scissors.
Well, that escalated quickly…
Don't you worry…

These were elementary scissors, and they were not sharp at all. She didn't bleed or anything, but I did get sent to the office. I know it sounds horrible, but I knew I wasn't Ted Bundy or anything. I just had uncontrollable *Bitch-dom*. So, I'm forgiven.

(Bitch-Dom: /biCH/dem/ (Noun) Entering the Stage of Being A Bitch)

I needed to defend myself. There could have been thousands of other ways to do it, but I didn't know them yet.

I was lucky to leave my mean-Bitch friends years after, though. And soon after leaving my mean Bitch friends, I found a good Bitch.

A Badass Bitch.

She was the one who told me to stand up for myself. While people kept telling me to continue following orders, she instead asked me what I loved and wanted. She helped me without hesitation and invited me in when no others would have done so.

Her name is Andrea (Real name. She won't sue me...I think). Years of pent-up aggression took a toll on me, and I found myself crying at the corner bus stop one day after high school. Andrea didn't ask what was wrong; she simply hugged me. She also didn't expect answers. Maybe she knew I didn't have them myself. She just understood that I needed to let it out.

She stared at me and said, "Cry." And so, I did.

But I was still frustrated. *Why was I so dumb?*

I had swallowed the feelings of being used. I had devoured my loneliness, silenced the empty feeling of knowing the few friends I had would dump me the next day if I said something the wrong way. I had to find reasons for why I was a Dumb Bitch and why I wanted to leave the "Dumb" part of that sentence.

And here was the big picture: I had a psychotic boyfriend, no real friends, no social life, and no character. I was emotionally abused in friendships, felt like a loner inside my family, and lost the few good people I had in my life. On top of that, I was overweight and no one to talk to.

But why?

Why did I let that happen?

I had to (in simple terms) face the truth.

Who, what, where, and how?

What hurt me before that I allowed such idiocy to take over? Who hurt me, and why couldn't I deal with the present? Where could I go for help if I needed it?

Not to mention, I had bottled up secrets that I couldn't even tell my family. Instead of dealing with those issues, they became dark clothes, black makeup, and short hair: short enough to look like Kobe Bryant when having an afro.
I thought holding my emotions in wouldn't affect me at all.

But shit, I was wrong!

I thought I had arrived at Bitch-Dom, but I went too far off the rails. My Bitch-Dom was left waiting at the dock, and I went swimming into chaos.
I became a Crazy Ass Bitch.
Dumb Bitch sounded far better.

And because I ignored my issues, I found myself in a rut years later: Single motherhood: broke, no job, no man, no hope.

I found myself scrambling for money at one point because I couldn't feed my baby. I gathered money any way I could, and when everything was paid for, I looked at my bank account, and my balance was eleven cents.

That felt like shit.

I thought I was the worst mother ever to exist. And then again, back at the bottom. The train dropped me off at Dumb-Bitch Hood once again.

It was now time to figure this all out and crawl out of the hole I dug for myself.

Face the truth: Be honest with yourself.

My car was a piece of shit (mostly my fault). I left college, and I couldn't even walk up and talk to my mom, let alone my sisters. The rotten cherry on top was a "friend" who had me in arguments with my older sister, whom I felt was my motherly figure. And I didn't even have that anymore.

I felt that isolated.

But Wait…

I did have someone.

I had my inner Bitch.

The only value I had then was my voice, and I had a fire inside my asshole screaming at me to

WAKE THE FUCK UP!

What caused me to wake up? If I had been shut down for years, what causes someone to have a fire up their asshole?

For me, it was something so simple:

We were out having dinner one night. My mom and friend had invited my ex-boyfriend and me to have Mexican food. I was up to my ass in constant arguments. I was fed up with him finding any little excuse not to work or not to provide money for the bills we both had accumulated.

He began complaining that he didn't want Mexican food. I said the restaurant had other options. Once he found that the different options weren't to his liking, he began complaining about everything I was doing: The way I was eating, the way I was moving, how I was holding my tortillas, how my plate looked, and he even said that my food looked like "Dog Shit" *(his words, not mine)*.

"THEN GO SOMEWHERE ELSE AND PAY FOR YOUR FUCKING FOOD!"

The eruption in my chest began as a cold shiver and then hot to my face. I wasn't happy with the way I said it, nor the words I chose to say. Maybe I could have been respectful, but at that time, I wasn't so sure how to even vocalize thoughts and feelings.

But what slapped me in my face was my friend's words. After he stormed out of the restaurant, I kept staring at my food in embarrassment, and then I heard these magical words, *"Wow, Welcome back,"*

And BOOM!

I was slapped out of a *Dumbfuckery.*

(Dumbfuckery: /dem/fek/UH-rie/ (Vulgar, Slang) The State of Being a Fucking Dumbass!) Exclamation point included in the definition.

I realized I hadn't been myself for years. He chose what I wore. He chose who I hung out with. He chose practically every aspect of my character. And because of that, I had become someone I hated. Someone I wasn't happy with. My friend was right.

My inner Bitch finally came out.

Finding your inner Bitch is about going through memories and emotions to discover what has been keeping your inner Bitch hidden.

Some of us have our inner Bitch on the surface with access to her whenever we need her, and that's awesome. But if you don't, do you feel you will burst out as I did back then? Or maybe you have already? Think about that for a second. Are you holding feelings inside that are making you unhappy? What are ways you can express yourself and not bottle every feeling inside? Because trust me, it feels horrible to keep your inner self locked up.

PostScript: My ex-boyfriend purchased Subway next door and survived my inner Bitch's retaliation. And adding to the plus, he bought his own food!

We went home, and I went straight into my closet. I pulled out all my spring dresses with huge fucking flowers on them (*I hated them*). I took my phone and texted my best friend (*which he hadn't allowed me to for months*). I counted all the money spent and gathered all the things I had purchased to sell them (*we needed money*).

And after arguing for a long time, I had to turn the mirror unto myself. I had to excavate as to why I had allowed this to happen again, just like my elementary friends, just like boyfriends who made me waste so much money and ended up leaving me in the end.

And after a proper search and rescue, I found I was trying to hide my childhood struggles with a pretty cheap curtain. I thought that keeping these feelings and struggles hidden, that no one would see them, and I was going to act all right, even though I was being murdered behind the scenes.

Now, I will not reveal secrets about my childhood just now because they are still working themselves out.

But as an adult, I understand why I was such an angry child. I know why I was a lonely girl, and while I would love to tell you, I am not so sure I have dealt with them enough to be brought up on broad daylight.

Those demons are drinking tea inside my head, and I'm sure, one day, I will walk in with a blowtorch and scorch the fucking place up.
But for now, we will call them *unfortunate events*.

However, this doesn't mean that I didn't write them down at one point or dealt with them. This doesn't mean I didn't think about them or spoke to a counselor. This doesn't mean I ignored them, no.

I am letting those demons drink tea because before, they had nothing but tequila.

This book isn't to understand my unfortunate events but to understand yours. And by understanding yours, you'll find those Bitch triggers that will make you yell at yourself in the third person:

(Insert Your Name Here)! WAKE THE FUCK UP!

As for me, one of my MANY Bitch triggers was fake people. People who gave themselves the labels of friends, best friends, acquaintances, boyfriends, and then turned around to backstab once I shifted a shoulder. My Bitch triggers were people who would take advantage, lie to my face, destroy my property or belongings as a joke, and left me paying the bill.

And I don't blame them. I can't. I was a people pleaser. So, I let them.

Now, I will drop in a disclaimer here and tell you that I, too, was a mean bitch at one point in my life. Not all the time, but sometimes. And I know my crazy Bitch hurt others. There were times where I could have been better and times where I shouldn't have treated people a certain way, but I was learning, and I fucked up a lot as well. I was trying to find peace inside an emotional war zone.

Most of the time, though, I was just trying to make everyone happy. Sometimes making someone happy made others sad, and I couldn't say anything. I just didn't know what to do, and I spread myself thin.

To this day, I catch myself doing that.

I still do it.

Unconsciously.

Why? I don't know.

Maybe years of practice. You know how the bike reference goes:

> *"Once one learns how to ride a bike, they can never forget it because it gets stored within the procedural memory."*

And I didn't even know what the fuck "Procedural memory" was!

I had to dive into the pool of pleaser dumbfuckery to find out if it was just my environment, my unfortunate events, or even just my culture.

Maybe a savory combination of all.

Moving from Mexicali, Mexico, to Pomona, California, ripped apart my happiness. It tore me apart from a life I loved. And most of all, it pulled me from whom I loved the most: my cousins.

I remember I wasn't allowed to go to school with my cousin one morning because we were leaving. I still remember the color of the car I was holding onto, the dirt-paved road, and looking at the car, going at a distance with my cousin inside it looking back.

Isn't that so movie-friendly?

Fuck yeah!

I am dramatic, so bear with my imagination.

One of my cousins, Nicknamed Cachito, would always come over during the summer. He and I were inseparable (He was the one I was crying for when leaving Mexico). Although I was harsh with him and somewhat a mean Bitch, he loved me, and I did him.

Summers were filled with trips to the pool, trips to Six Flags, the beach, the mountains, and eating. Even inside my home, we always had things to do. Summer was it.

Then school came, and shit, I was lonely again. My school friends never translated to outside school, and the one friend I made was in another grade. The friends who translated out of school always put me in dangerous and unfortunate situations, so I stayed home.

When I did find someone, I would stick to them like Krazy glue on a lego. I didn't want to share them. I was too afraid of losing the one friend I had, so I people pleased them in hopes of them never leaving me. But it would hurt terribly when they set me aside for someone else.

As for culture, I am Mexican American, and I can tell you that Mexican parents have this beautiful thing they do when someone comes around:

"Look, Mija, she is your age and has a house already,"
"He bought himself a Corvette and finished school at 22,"
"She is married and has two kids. When are you getting married?"

So my struggle was trying to make sure everyone was OK with my choices, even school friends. And because I was never "the skinny one," "The smart one," or "The funny one," I ended up trying to please everyone and everything at my expense.

I call this our "Mommy Look! Syndrome"

We have to make sure people are content with our decisions. We have to make sure they are OK with our boyfriends, our lives, our cars, and everything before moving onto the next thing. We have this "Mommy, Look! Syndrome engraved that it has made Instagram, Snapchat, TikTok, and other apps a considerable success. We crave the likes, the approvals, the applause emoticons, and we stop at nothing to get them. By the way, if you wanna follow my Instagram, links will be provided later.

Lol. No joke.

Now, it's your turn.

I want you to find your triggers. I want you to find your inner child, inner feelings and get them to the surface. Face them. They are scary, but it's a step in the right direction.

Because when you find them, you can catch yourself when you're doing something that isn't good for you, and that's the trick. By seeing yourself, you begin to control what Dumbfuckeries you're falling into.

Hell yeah, you're going to catch yourself!

We will catch ourselves many times. It is part of our subconscious, and that Bitch is hidden behind the curtains at all times. And remember, when you do. Acknowledge it, regain and let it go. When I catch myself, I don't dwell on it. I don't obsess over the why. I simply acknowledge it and move on because I know where it comes from.

But we do have to revisit the past to understand the present.

People always say to ignore the past, but it is there where you will find yourself, and it is there where you will find your inner Bitch hidden behind the closet corner.

WHAT TO DO

NOTE: For years, I have been giving my spiritual clients this advice. This work is not necessarily spiritual but an emotional work intended for yourself and your inner feelings. Those who have taken the time to do it have found themselves understanding certain aspects of their life that they didn't know before.

****If you find yourself dealing with trauma and something you cannot handle by yourself, please consult a therapist/counseling as they are much more educated to handle this****

www.mentalhealth.gov

www.samhsa.gov (Substance Abuse and Mental Health Services)

www.nami.org (Natural Alliance on Mental Illness)

1.   On a piece of paper, write the names of people who have hurt you or maybe that you have hurt instead.

2.   Write a number next to their name (1 being the lowest of hurt to 5 being the highest)

3.   For those with the highest numbers, I want you to write them a letter. Be as detailed as possible. What happened? Why does it continue to hurt you, and what do you want to say? *No one will read the letter, so be as detailed as possible.* You will notice that sometimes when you open up your feelings to a particular situation, you will begin to uncover feelings or things you didn't know existed before.

4.   Feel your emotions. If you feel like crying, do it. If you feel like singing, do it. Sometimes, speaking out loud and talking things through helps. Scream, sing, sleep, do something soothing, and release. *Do something nice for yourself, never hurtful.*

***I advise people to talk out loud. Your brain has this great thing: if you speak out loud, it listens to itself more so than silent. READ the letter out loud. Sometimes, it works if you're in front of a mirror.

Be prepared to let it go. It took me seven years to finally do this exercise because I was not ready to let it go.

*I wanted to find answers; I wanted to hear apologies from someone else until I understood **it was within me to move on.** <u>It was not in the hands of someone else.</u>*

****When you are ready to let it go, you feel it is time to move on, **erase the letter, burn it, rip it, shred it.***

> *Let it go.*
>
> *You do not need those emotions anymore.*
>
> 5.   As for those people with three or less, ask
>
> yourself why you feel bothered or hurt by them.
>
> Will it ever increase to more than three? If it
>
> doesn't, should you even bother adding them to
>
> your daily worries? If you can let it go, do it.
>
> Otherwise, consider adding another star and
>
> repeat the steps above.

The challenging part here is that people expect an actual

apology from the person itself. You can't put expectations

on someone else. You will only make yourself unhappy.

This exercise is to heal your inner self; it is not to reform

those old school Bitches who hurt you. I also don't suggest

camping out with water balloons, glitter bombs, or

envelopes filled with cow shit, no.

This exercise is to hear yourself. Listen to that hurting heart, listen to that silenced inner Bitch.

I want you to feel like you have uncovered some reason why you feel the need to bring out your inner Bitch. Understanding your Inner Bitch is truly a stepping stool to understanding your Outer Bitch.

One on one. At peace with the world.

Chapter 2: Your Bitch Influencer

Walking into Tower Records (An old school record store), I stumbled across one of the end caps "New Best Sellers" albums of the month. This was pre-Apple music, pre-Spotify, pre-YouTube music.

Fuck! I'm old.

At the corner end cap, a cover with an image of this girl caught my attention. Her black hair, fair light skin covered in tattoos posing with her eyes up was way too cool for me, but I picked it up anyway.

The first song on the record, "Beauty Fiend," started, and I picked up the headset to preview the album right away. I was hooked. This band, called My Ruin, spoke to my inner feelings.

34

Lyrics such as "I've got demons inside me and sometimes they need to speak" and "At my calmest I'm tired of explaining how it feels," were shooting straight up into my soul. Then her fantastic screaming roar said, "My mouth as always is brutally honest," and I knew then, in one song, that I had found my badass Bitch influencer: Tairrie B.

She spoke of shit I was just writing about in my journal. She expressed her truth, and it didn't matter who heard it. I began researching her persona. I was fond of her lyrics, her voice, and herself. It took one song for me to realize that I wanted to be like her.

I purchased the album without hesitation, and sixteen years later, I still want some My Ruin-Esque tattoo on my body. I followed her albums, purchased those she did before forming My Ruin, and even met her a couple of times at shows (not to brag, but she invited me backstage several times for a photoshoot and a meet-up). I am that much of a fangirl.

I'm not saying buy a My Ruin album, though they are pretty kick-ass if you're into metal. I am merely telling you to be influenced by someone.

What is your goal to achieve Bitch-dom?

Do you want to feel powerful?

Do you want to feel loved?

Do you want to love yourself?

Find someone that matches your belief system, and there you go. Read on them, be influenced by them. Watch that I am saying "Influenced" and not "Being Jealous" of them. I don't envy Tairrie B. I don't want her exact life. I don't want her husband (though Mick Murphy is plenty hot). Tairrie B has a fantastic persona. Her attitude, her thoughts, and her creativity inspire on the daily.

I will warn you that your influencers will also make mistakes and change belief systems. When that time comes, I can pick and choose and move on. I am not going to throw myself off a bridge if Tairrie B does as well. I might stare at a distance and ponder her decision because, as a Bitch Influencer, I will learn from her greatness as well as her mistakes, if there are any.

Now, if you choose Hitler as a Bitch Influencer, I might suggest going to talk to a therapist on why. I, myself, will stay clear of hurtful people—just an FYI.

Choose someone that will inspire you. Find someone who brings out the best in you. And when they make mistakes, don't mimic them. Simply learn from them and do not assume life has to be black and white. If whatever they are doing seems wrong, you can choose their good parts and continue.

Please do not find yourself stuck inside a cult-like environment where you feel the need to follow your Bitch-Influencer's every word. Religion is a great example. *(oooh, yes, I went there!)*

Often, religious groups take things too seriously and make their followers judge and hate without reason or compassion.

Use common sense and respect.

Those who have understood that a higher power is simply loving and respect live peacefully, in no fear, and are always respectful to every Religion.

38

And before you go into a church tantrum, I have met people like that. I have met a Christian who is overcritical, won't speak to someone who wears a pentacle, and walks by wishing they had holy water to throw at passing Pagans. On the other hand, I have also met a Christian who is the most generous person I've ever met.

And by the way, I also met Satanists who were the sweetest people I've ever known. Their Religion doesn't matter to me. What matters is the respect they had for me. Extremists help no one.

Respect does.

A couple of years ago, Tairrie B chose to stay off social media for a couple of months. Her page went on standstill; she didn't update her merchandise web, and she rarely posted even a photo of herself.

Did I shut my stuff down? No.

Did I judge her for it? No.

She has been in the limelight of our glory for years, even before I began following her that it was time for her to say, "I need a break." And assuming my thoughts were correct, I continued.

Was I going to stop following her? No.

Did I erase all her albums off my Spotify? Hell no!

I simply understood what she meant. She wanted to focus on a social media-free life, and I don't blame her. Social media can be truly stressful. By the way, I took a weekend off, drove to Sacramento, and stayed away from social media myself.

And it was very refreshing.

Chapter 3: To Give a Fuck

The Art of Being a Bitch is not giving a fuck about things that people will say to you or about you, especially if that person isn't someone you would take any life advice from. Trust me when I tell you this.

As a person who spent her first 20 fucking years of life caring about every little fucking comment, every look, every word someone said, it is not cool. And yes, I am using the word "Fucking" a lot because that's the exact feeling.

I cared about everything everyone said.

I cared about every stare.

I cared about every measly little second of my life that it was daunting just to keep waking up.

If you don't know me, let me tell you... I love singing. I have done it since I was a baby. I used to sit in recess and sing by myself as I stared at all the other kids playing with their friends (Mary Poppins shit). My dad bought me a radio when I was four, a karaoke machine when I was six, and I loved it. There are several recorded videos and cassettes to prove how much I did.

Sadly, when something happened to me, I reverted inward. The person who hurt me made it clear that they wouldn't believe me if I were to tell someone because I was young, stupid, and the family's black sheep.

My vocal cords shriveled into tiny atoms and shut down. My karaoke machine went into the garage and my cassettes into storage. Suddenly, I didn't want the limelight anymore.

Not to mention, I had no real friends in school to talk to, so I simply shut the fuck up. For years...

When I attempted to speak, to vocalize, to show up, I was shut down again. Hundreds of kids rolled their eyes at me during a poem recital. I'm sure they did that with every kid, but I took it personally. I took it the worst.

This affected me with many relationships. I could never speak up. I could never break up or break away from hurtful people. An ex-boyfriend called me after a break-up, telling me he was looking for a rope to hang himself, so I stayed in a painful relationship. A friend of mine told me she wanted us to run away, even to the point of getting in a car, and I didn't say anything. Another friend tried to leave me alone with someone much older than I was. My car was crashed by someone else, and I took the blame.

These are just a few examples of how I let friends backstab me in plain sight, and I never spoke up. I said nothing. Sad but true.

I took all the blame, and I took all the issues inward to protect them because it was better to get in trouble myself than to point fingers and voice them out.

But now, I sing in front of people (it only took me years of attempts, diarrhea impacted threats, and karaoke bar walkouts for that but still), I do it proudly and sometimes horribly. I put myself out there: my art, work, and the most significant thing: *I speak the truth.*

I talk to someone as honestly as I can. Sure, sometimes, I can sound rude and piss off a few people, but I am everyday evolving, like Pokemon. *So, cue the Pokemon theme song.*

After the Dog-Shit dinner my ex-boyfriend and I had, and after I cleared out my closet of the horrible clothing, I texted my best friend. It was a release being able to speak to her as I did before. I knew she had her walls up, but I was ready and dedicated to knocking them down gently.

Concerning the relationship with my ex, I was able to voice my thoughts and feelings when things needed to be done. I was not disrespectful, though. I simply needed him to get a stable job and pay for half of our responsibilities. And because he was used to not doing anything, he began getting mad, even when we both lived in the same home, and both had accumulated a couple of bills.

Even now, I get called a Bitch for both positive and negative comments. Sometimes, I find myself thinking out loud, and my friends get a little tense and bothered. I am not looking for trouble, but I do voice when my mind speaks. If they disagree, we talk, sometimes argue. If it's regarding a joke, we laugh. But I am always respectful, ask any of them.

So dear friends, bear with me as I bear with you.

The remarkable thing about not giving a fuck is knowing that, in the end, you will live with yourself. You sleep inside your brain. You wear what makes you feel comfortable, and you act as good as you make yourself feel.

Before the end, when the grim reaper is at your bedside, you will not think of Ana, who told you, you once looked weird in that neon sweater. You won't think of Freddy, who rolled his eyes when you colored your hair that bright purple pink. When death is nearside, you will think of how you were in your own life and the many things you wanted to do or say but couldn't.

Live your life how you want. Make yourself happy.

Don't live in the expectations of others.

We live in a world where we think normalcy is getting a

career by twenty-two, getting a house by twenty-five,

married by twenty-seven, kids by thirty, retirement at sixty-

five, and death by eighty.

Trust me when I tell you this that is complete **BULLSHIT!**

It is OK to get married at 50.

It is OK to have a kid at 35

It is OK to complete school at 36.

It is OK if you purchase your home at 47.

If you weren't able to get it sooner, then stop beating

yourself up for it. At least you got around to it. If you got it

done before, that's fine too. Each person's path is different,

and no one will ever be the same. Stop comparing yourself

to the normalcy of the media and movies telling you it is otherwise.

It rarely is.

But if you ask Normal Joe, that is what should be done, and if you don't get it done, judgment day is upon you, and you should hate yourself.

But fear not.

In the end, it is about you and making yourself happy. So choose what you give a fuck about.

For example, I care about my son. I care about my dog. I care about my nephews, nieces, and my entire family. But when it comes to my personal life, I have to choose for myself. Sure, I will adjust, compromise, and find middle-grounds, but I decided that at the end of the day.

Not them.

One of my sisters hates tattoos. She says they're cheap, and she would never do that with her body. On the other hand, I have six (I assume 10+ by the time I reach forty). I believe that tattoos are a way of writing a story. It is a permanent art form on your body. My sister and I are different.
Is she wrong? No.
Am I wrong? No.

She just believes something else, and that's perfectly fine. I have to pick and choose what judgment I take from her. Yes, I care about her and give a fuck about her, but in the end, her belief system is different than mine, so I can't even bother. If I choose to base my give-a-fucks on her belief systems, I will be unhappy all the time.

People will always criticize, comment, stare, and judge. That is the world we live in, and I blame American Idol-Esque shows for that. We live in a world filled with mean judges, and people thrive on negative criticism because it makes good TV. This is why we have YouTube riddled with Fail videos, Caught on Cameras, and saturation of Judging shows on TV.

But that doesn't even fly under my radar.

Because I choose for me.

People who talk the most are the ones that least know you. They assume horribly and never ask questions. But I don't give a fuck. I want to make myself happy first. Of course, responsibly and respectfully. So, please stop worrying about what others think. Stop being nervous about living your own life.

Wear what you love.

Sing out loud.

Listen to whatever you want.

Paint your room green!

You will be nervous at first, but it will get better in time.

First-timers always are. If you visit a nudist colony, you'd

be embarrassed at first. But after a few tries, trust me, you'll

be walking around, saggy boobs and balls about.

Most often than not, people don't give a fuck what you're

doing. They just like to talk shit, so let them.

We all had first jobs, first kisses, first sexual experiences,

first speeches, first everything. We have all been there.

If we see someone rolling their eyes inside a crowd, we

assume everyone is doing that to us. That one person

changes everything for you. So don't let it.

Remember when I said kids rolled their eyes at my poem

recital? It was probably just a group of five kids, but I

pictured everyone doing it. I imagined everyone hating me.

I saw imaginary tomatoes hitting the stage, splashing onto

my thrift store shoes and polka-dot sweater.

In actuality, it was kids who knew I was stuck inside a

Dumbfuckery, and they loved to make me feel

embarrassed. Just as all kids do nowadays, but to me, it was

the end of days, and Thanos had snapped his fingers right

into my pride and love for show-business.

We can't continue to overgeneralize the feelings of the

entire population. We will live inside a box if we do. We

are all weirdos, people! Tattoos or not, **we are**. People love

quoting The Craft. When the girls are standing outside the

bus, Nancy Downs (one of the witches) says, "We are the

weirdos, mister." And it makes me wonder. She's

somewhat correct. The entire fucking population is weird.

We are all weird in different ways.

Part of life's normality.

Choose your give-a-fucks and keep that to a minimum. Human beings are far too busy to be worrying about everything and everyone. We set ourselves up for anxiety and depression when we base our life on other's expectations and belief systems. That isn't good for our health, any health: mental, physical, you name it.

I often judge people on Instagram who use extra glossy, stretch skin filters, but I think it's more a disappointment than judgment. I love people who show who they are, and I think I get annoyed when someone says, "I look better with filters than showing my real face because of my scars, pimples, or wrinkles, etc." But I love seeing scars, pimples, freckles, and the raw look of our natural beauty.

But fuck me, right?
In the end, it's your Instagram and not mine.

Fuck me.

Throw me off the curve and roll me off the cliff. Shoot those Snapchats however you want and however many you feel like. I encourage you to flip me off when I post a meme about filters.

But remember, it's my Instagram, and I do what I want there. *So Fuck You too.*

Chapter 4: It's OK to be a weak Bitch.

Have you ever flipped the channel and come across the ASPCA commercial with the saddened dogs inside their incarcerated cages? I never watched that commercial before knowing I have plenty of ice cream inside my freezer for those fifteen seconds of emotional eating. Does that paint a picture of me? No?

Let me give you another example.

Remember that scene of Dumb and Dumber where they both cry at the Pacific Bell commercial, and they wipe their tears and noses with hundred-dollar bills?

That's me.

Minus the $100 bills.

I am known to be a very emotional person.

Dramatic for sure too, but emotional as shit.

For years, I have been stared at when something emotional happens. People look at me because they know, WaterWorld is about to come on. They turn and stare. Often accompanied by "Are you crying already?"

If I wanna be emotional, I am! I don't have to act "tough" when something emotional comes on. Who wants to be that fake? I like keeping my emotions on the surface rather than keeping them sunk into the abyss of self-loathing.
That's me, and I feel no shame. Not anymore.
I am just saying it is OK to cry.
We need it.

Crying releases those bottled-up emotions, and it lets out stressors of everyday life. Remember when I said that I cried at a bus stop back in high school? I had held my emotions in for years because it was always a sign of weakness if I cried. We grew up with the "tough it up!" culture. What they didn't realize is that keeping everything inside is terrible for us. It often results in people acting out, cutting, shootings, self-loathing, and depression.

Get it out there. Fucking let your emotions out, please! When you feel like crying, do so. Really. Throw on some good fucking music and cry your ass off. It is good, and it feels good after. Holding those emotions in only causes you to bottle everything up, and that will tarnish you from the inside. And let me give some examples:

Fill a balloon with water and continue every day without stopping for ten years. Hold a fart in all day and continue holding it in every day without ever letting it go. Keep pressing the gas pump without stopping, overfilling your gas tank, and do not stop.

At one point, something is either going to burst, spill, or shit out all over. Emotions are the same. Keep filing your chest with feelings that cannot express themselves, and you'll find yourself exploding like a fart in the middle of the library.

It's gonna be loud. And you don't want that.

You wanna cry because you remembered what happened back on October 10th, 1999?

Cry.

You want to cry because you stubbed your toe in the bed and realized you chipped your freshly pedicured nails?

Cry.

You want to cry because you saw sunlight beaming nicely upon the forest meadow?

Cry!

And after you cried a perfect cry, remember, it is time to get back up. It is time to put on that badass Bitch utility belt and start knocking down some doors. Know that it is OK to feel weak and strong the next day.

It is OK to be both.

You have the right to continue. You have the right to throw in the towel and get back up the next day. But please remember: Always get back up.

I promise shit gets better.

I have seen people refuse to get up. I have seen someone I loved turned to alcoholism. I had to drag him off the street one night because he said he wanted to get run over by a car. I had to sit and remain silent as he allowed himself to succumb to his emotional cocoon. I was honestly waiting for that butterfly to flap its wings one day, but it's the year 2019, and I am still waiting.

I also saw someone turn to hardcore drugs. A beautiful boy dazed out in the middle of the park because he had forgotten how to get home. I saw his adorable face turn sour as the years went by, and the last time I heard, he was worse.

I have heard about attempted suicides and self-hurt from people I grew up with.

Please don't do that, just keep getting up: Mentally, Physically, Emotionally.

Life is going to get better.

And while I do not have the authority to walk you through as a professional therapist would, I can surely provide references and links to where to go for help. *(See previous links listed in Chapter 1)*

As for mini guidance, I would suggest that if you have a friend, talk to them. Ask them to listen like Andrea did to me. Ask them not to question but to listen. Sometimes, that's all we need. And remember, you have the right to feel emotions. You have the right to feel sad, happy, joyful, stressed, angry, embraced, loved, disgusted, annoyed, excited, and all the other emotions I couldn't name in thirty seconds.

When Captain Marvel looked so endearingly at Stan Lee during his cameo, my friend Liz looked at me and said, "I feel like crying, but that's OK because I'm on my period. Are you on your period?"

I said no.

"Oh, so you're just a weak Bitch,"

And we laughed our asses off.

We are so used to accepting emotions only when we are on our periods, but it seems I'm on my period year-round if you ask all my friends. And that's OK! We don't need reasons to feel emotions. We just do. We don't need a reason to be emotional. We just are.

We are human beings that periodically change moods because the world changes as well. If mother nature wants to give us chirping birds and tornadoes the next day, she does. That's how humans are. Imagine an interconnected avatar in Pandora. *(God, where is my Jake Sully?)* And if things are simply not going your way, that's perfectly OK, too. That is just life's many misadventures, and someday, it is going to piece itself together and back out again.

Life cannot and will never be perfect.

And that's perfectly imperfect.

If I feel I want a good scream fest, if I feel like singing mariachi with Vicente Fernando, cry for the one who got away and pass out in the open arms of my best friend, then fuck yeah, I'll do that! So bring on the tequila!

It is far too much work to be tough at all times. I didn't realize that being tough and weak at the same time is perfectly normal. During some of my darkest moments, I not only felt bad for feeling bad, but I hated myself for not being able to get back up. So, there was further hate on top of the hate. People call that spiraling out of control, but I was more of a natural disaster during a demolition. Flying debris of emotions kept splattering and killing every intent of ever feeling good.

Until one day, I had an Ah-HAH moment. I realized I had to be OK with being in a bad place.

And **BOOM!**

I suddenly felt a little hope. So what did I do? I cried. I cried a lot: nose snot and everything.

I even stood in front of the mirror, where you see yourself, makeup running through the cheeks, very cinematic looking cry, asking God the many Whys of my life, and then waited for my Oscar nomination.

I did that, and I felt good, even when the Academy Awards wasn't knocking on my door.

I understood I was OK, even when I was broken.

It is OK not to be OK.

Cliche phrase with lots of meaning.

If the issues you find yourself in are way worse and you feel you are suffocating, please get some help. It is OK to ask for help. There are tons of resources where you can find help if simply venting isn't enough. There is always a solution, and there is always someone who wants to listen.

Chapter 5: Don't Be a Dumb Bitch

In my many teachings of being a Bitch, I advise staying clear of being a Dumb Bitch. Don't be a Bitch if you just think it's cool to be an ass. Treating someone like shit for the sake of being funny is not the Art of Being A Bitch... you, my friend, are just an asshole.

A stinky one too.

Some Dumb Bitches do not understand the meaning of respect. Whether it is by giving it or receiving it. Do not find yourself stuck within the Dumbfuckeries of being a Bitch. Here are a minimal few:

The **"Entitled Bitch"**: We live in a world where female power is growing. I admire that women are getting tighter with respect, voicing their opinions, and looking for hammers to break that glass ceiling in many aspects of their lives. However, just because you feel tough doesn't mean you must hate and disrespect all men and women that are in your way.

Entitled Bitches always complain when they are not getting what they want, at the exact moment they want it. For example, when someone is walking in front, they demand people to move to the side instead of moving to themselves.

And don't get me started with some female drivers: when someone is walking or bicycling, the entitled Bitch will drive close to the person just because they need to stand their ground. No, Dumb Bitch, no. Move to the next lane, slow down a bit, and move away from a person when you are driving a vehicle.

Look, I get it.

You fought yourself up the ladder, and you are at a point in time where you feel you don't need to bend your arm, but we are all sharing this world. It doesn't revolve around your big ass head.

When someone opens a door for you, don't yell at them not to. Don't roll your eyes and say you don't need anyone to help you. On the opposite spectrum, don't demand everyone to open doors for you. It does not matter who the fuck opened the Godamn door: old, young, fat, skinny, white, black, female, male... say thank you and keep going. Don't be a dumb Bitch.

The **"Exactly-Like-You Bitch"** Have you ever been with a girl who tries to fit in, even to the point of ass-kissing or mimicking everything you like and do?

Yes. We all have.

To be a great Bitch, you have to be true to yourself. Don't be the "cool" girl, the "goth" girl, the "science" girl, the "horror" girl if you aren't. Don't be fake, that's it! Being a great Bitch doesn't accept fakeness.

"Oh, I love the Rolling Stones even before my boyfriend said he did."
"Oh, yes, I was into death gore since I was six, even before Horror became popular three years ago."
 No, Dumb Bitch. No.

The beauty of common sense is that we can spot a fake Bitch miles away. Especially if you know people for years.

People told me they love death metal when I've known them for twenty years, and not once have they ever put a death metal song on.

Don't try to fit in.

You'll find your puzzle piece without a struggle. We will love you for who you are: death metal or no death metal.
I always get an internal laugh when someone is fake. Now, I laughed internally because my job is to stay clear of fake Bitches, not to beam light on them. Frankly, I don't have time to be a Bitch to them when I can be a great Bitch somewhere else.

That's not my job... yet.

Krys for President. Make it happen.

The Repetition-Bitch: Now, this type of Dumb Bitch, I honestly cannot pinpoint if this is by conditioning or by choice. This type of Bitch is someone who keeps stepping on the same stone for years, even after knowing what the stone is and what it does.

For example, let's call this girl Ana.

Ana has been dating this guy for years. He takes advantage of her. He tells her shit that no one should be telling her, and she says nothing back. Ana takes everything in because she doesn't want to let him go. She doesn't want to be alone and is in fear of break-ups.

I am not talking about physical abuse or extreme verbal abuse (please, if you are going through that, seek help.) Just some jerk being disrespectful. But Ana remains there.

Ana never speaks. Ana has become a Dumb Bitch. Why? Because the first rule of Bitch-dom is to demand respect, respectfully.

Now, here is a fine line between someone being a jerk and a partner. If you are married and you are in a happy relationship if your husband or boyfriend says something rude once or you guys fight over bills, make sure this isn't just typical bickering between partners. Having fights, miscommunication, and disagreements is a normal part of relationships, and they always happen.

Living with your partner is tough, and shit's are gonna happen. The true Bitch will calm down, live through the argument, decide or undecide, and continue living the next day. If you are one of those people that looks for a perfect relationship, someone who will never argue or never face obstacles, let me buy you a cat already because you're never going to find anyone.

And as much as people say,

"I'd rather be alone,"

"I'm happy being alone forever," it's not true, and please, be honest with yourself.

I am talking about relationships. You know what, even friendships where one person is insulting and hurtful without contempt to the other. I am talking about relationships you know are a dead end, and you don't want to leave because you're afraid of the break-up process or because you don't want to hurt this jerk's feelings.
As humans, we know exactly when a relationship has no future. We feel it in our butthole, really deep in there like a suppository.

We know. We just don't want to admit it. Or, if we do, we don't want to do anything about it for many reasons: loneliness, confrontation, embarrassment, fear.

This is where I say that I am not sure if this is conditioning or just dumbfuckery. We all had terrible relationships. And if you haven't, you might find yourself in one later, so no judging.

But the great thing about being a badass Bitch is that we get out of it soon enough. I don't know if my future boyfriends will be dicks, or losers, or great, or badass, but I know I will choose for myself.

If I fuck up, great. Another thing to learn.

If I make it, great, I am already here.

In the process, it is up to the person itself to be removed from the Dumbfuckery.

Not their parents.

Not their peers.

Not their coworkers.

Don't let anyone dictate your Dumbfuckery if you're in one, but do understand when you simply aren't happy anymore. If you change, adapt, or compromise, good. If not, then it's time to let the Dumbfuckery go.

Chapter 6: Be a Boss Bitch

I love management, and I love bossing people around (for lack of better words). I always found myself managing a department or being in a supervising position. At one point, I had more access than the boss' wife (not sexually), and it felt great. I have been a human resources manager, accounting head, office manager, head cashier, and plumbing department manager.

But I left. I hated not making my schedule. I often repeat this mantra, and I keep it true to this day. "I don't want a boss." Of course, my mantra can change later. Who knows what will happen when my kid goes off to college, but as of now: *I. Do. Not. Want. A. Boss.*

That is what I'm working towards.

Now, when it comes to being a boss Bitch, I do not mean
that to be a Boss Bitch, you will have to make your
schedule or be your own boss.

No.

What being a boss Bitch means to me is that you genuinely
find something you love to do and work your fucking best
at it.

Do you want to be the corporation's best accountant? Boss
Bitch it.

Do you want to work at a pet shelter to be surrounded by
tons of animals?

Be the boss Bitch there.

Do you want to be a lawyer?

Boss Bitch that shit.

I am saying work your ass off to become the best at what you love to do.

If you want to become an artist, a writer, an illustrator, a teacher, a manager, own your own business, become a CPA, then make sure you have plan A in motion but that you have plan B, C, D, and E… just in case not.

Being a boss Bitch means focusing on your dream job, working your ass off to pay your bills, taking care of yourself and your duties.

I used to work almost ten to twelve hours a day, Monday through Friday. My dedication was my work. I would even take work home, and I loved it. However, I found myself losing the mom battle at home. My son was having issues at school, and he was sleeping late and sleeping even at school.

78

I realized my "Boss Bitch" was a "Dumb-Mom Bitch," and I had to take action quickly. Not only that, but I was working hard at a job where I wasn't appreciated or even compensated appropriately. My previous manager, who did nothing but instigate issues between the boss and us, focused her hours flirting with the boys inside the warehouse, got compensated much more than I was when I took over her job. Not to mention the responsibilities were much higher when I was the manager.

I was more of a glorified Dwight Schrute from The Office: Acting manager of ABC Incorporated.

I realized I had stepped into a Dumbfuckery again. Fuck. Again? Yes. Like I said before, we will step into a Dumbfuckery many times in life, but the trick here is to catch yourself and make decisions.

As for me, I had options:

Work unhappily, continuing feeling underappreciated and under-compensated. Speak up, state my concerns and ask for the change or quit

While I loved my job, I loved the people I worked with, and I love the driving distance from home to work. However, I also knew that my future there was capped. If I were to stay, it would be only for the perks of having my own office and continuing bossing people around as I loved.

But I chose to leave. While I could have burned my bridges, I remained silent in the end. Instead, I slipped into my world, dedicating time to my kid and finding solutions to replace the income I had cut in half.

Being a boss Bitch means you demand respect within your workplace or get out. Being a boss Bitch means you make shit happen, and fear not. You can even be a boss Bitch when you have no employment. Full-time motherhood and full-time housewiving are challenging enough. So be a boss Bitch, and get shit done.

Being a boss Bitch also means you understand that not everything is going to work out as planned. It means we will wake up one day to burning toast, a flat tire, a loss of a job, a loss of sales, a broken phone, a fired friend, a lost record book, and stolen merchandise. We simply sigh and look forward to the next day.

Sometimes, I go to my events and make forty-five dollars. Do I throw in the towel and call it quits? No. Because as every entrepreneur will tell you, we will make one hundred a day or ten thousand. We will lose a client one day and gain ten the next month. That's just business. And we continue.

The Boss Bitch will shrug her shoulders, acknowledge the roadblock, and try again the next day. If you find yourself losing money, losing investments, if you find that what you're doing makes you happy no longer, the Boss Bitch will take that with a smile and move onto the next thing.

Finally, the boss Bitch criticizes no one and never flaunts as a purpose to compare. I know people who have their master's degrees. Some of them have bought houses, and some of them have families (husband included). I also know people who aren't going to school, are not married and do not have houses yet.

Are these two groups different? No.

I am sure mainstream belief will tell you that the latter are losers and unmotivated, just because they do not have a mortgage or a wedding ring.

To some people, I should be married, have a 9-5 job, and have ten thousand dollars in bonds. I should work inside an office, hating the week, hoping to gain some speck of fun during Friday or Saturday night and do it all over until I am 65. They assume that because I tripped over broke-hood once, that I am a loser and that I don't have any of the above planned. So, I shrug my shoulders and let them talk out of their ass.

"A bachelors? Pfft! That's nothing! You need a masters. You need a doctorate. You need alienshinship proloctarate!" (A made-up word)

Do you often get criticized because you don't have a 9-5? Do you get criticized because you're a single mother, living at home, needing mom to babysit while you work? Do you get frowned upon because you chose not to continue graduate college? Do people judge you because you don't have the means to purchase a home yet?

Just know that these people judge because they grew up with a traditional mentality. Also, know that your way of living, your way of hustling, or making things happen makes them uncomfortable. They don't see themselves doing that, and therefore, they assume you are uncomfortable as well. Or maybe they wanted to become something they couldn't, and because they hated their experience and failed, they feel the need to stop you on your own goals because they are "scared for you."

They don't know you.
They don't need to know you or your goals.

The fact is no one needs to know what you do to handle shit. No one needs to know how much you make. No one needs to see if you're inside a happy marriage. No one needs to know your business other than the people you feel comfortable with sharing.

Be a Boss Bitch.

Let me show you.

To those who demand to know everything about your life so that they can compare or criticize: do this.

Within your fingers, there is a larger one right in the middle. Do me a favor and put that middle of the five fingers up and lower the others. Lift that middle finger towards the people who criticize because you are not at "their level," whatever the fuck that means.

There you go, you just became a Boss Bitch.

We live in an If-You-Got-It-Flaunt-It kind of world, and that's fine if you want to. The bad thing here is if you judge others because they don't have it. Just because you went for a degree doesn't mean everyone will benefit from it if they go after it. Just because you have a nice expensive car doesn't mean the person sporting a tiny Versa is less than you, and just because you chose certain things doesn't mean you are better than others, and it certainly doesn't mean they are better than you.

We are all different, and we will choose different lifestyles.

Now, Krys, you speak of not judging others and yet criticized your ex. Isn't that contradicting yourself? Well, choosing a partner means we were to fuse our lives in one. Sometimes, when you do that, you have to work together and have similar goals in the end, and when you want to be with someone who doesn't match your goals, that causes more conflict than a solution. If you are willing to work different paths and have different lifestyles, that's great. If you are not willing, it's OK to move on.

Chapter 7: Men Can Be Bitches Too

If you are holding this book and your boyfriend, husband, best male friend, male acquaintance, or merely a man who bought this book for the sake of the title, then this chapter is for you. Not that the entire book isn't for you either, but in this chapter, I am focusing on the male species: the penis-embargo, the dick-dom of the living.

Feel free to re-read this book and substitute the word Bitch with Pentch. Which is a made-up word for Penis and Bitch. Like the word Bitch, this book explains the different ways of using the word Bitch and when it is OK to be one.

So listen up, Pentches.

Make sure you choose to be the correct Pentch instead of the other. To be a Pentch means making shit happen. Like all the chapters above, I'd suggest you follow through with the exercises and take whatever helps you move forward. There isn't much explaining to do since the book is self-explanatory. However, the Pentch I am asking you not to be is the following:

I have seen men whine and complain in relationships because the girl doesn't put them first, even when having children. I know that taking care of each other's needs is essential in relationships but don't make the other feel bad for not having time every day for you.

When a girl is busy, don't make her feel bad when they need to get something else done. Don't play the victim game and use emotional triggers to make her feel less.

If you don't want to go out, but she does, don't call her after she has made plans with friends and cry that she left you.

Don't demand affection and then complain that she is too clingy. Don't get her mad on purpose for the sake of getting her mad. Don't Bitch about it to her family that you only get the worst of her and be the cause of why she is a bitch.

My ex once said he loved to get me mad just to make me "happy again," and when I turned up the Bitch-Dom with a slice of crazy, he revolted.

Uh... no. You don't choose our Bitch-dom levels.
Don't be a little Bitch.

Don't disrespect and then whine because you are being disrespected. On the other hand, don't act irresponsible and take advantage of her kindness.

At this moment, if you are a little Bitch, I'm sure you're going to close the book and say I don't know what I'm talking about. I am sure you will toss it inside the charity bin or the trash can and call me an idiot because I don't know what I'm talking about.

Words of advice: Please throw the book inside a recycle bin to help the planet somehow.

If you are upset, turn the mirror onto yourself and ask what you are doing and why this is getting you upset. If anything I am saying offends you, look into your inner self a little further. Now, if you have a girlfriend who is batshit crazy and hurts you, then I am not talking to you. This chapter can go both ways, just as respect should.
I am talking to the people who hurt on purpose and take advantage of someone else.

If you are those men who leave babies with different women and then pat your shoulders because you feel you did your best in society by passing your unwanted sperm across the universe: You're welcome. You are a little Bitch. If you judge others because their life isn't perfect, because they don't eat healthily, or because they don't work out: Congratulations, you are a little Bitch.

If you have a way of living and believe everyone else's living is bad and incorrect. Please remove your huge ass head out of your inertia ass and congratulate yourself: You are a little Bitch.

If you have been cheating on someone and lie to their face, telling them they're the worst, and they're the ones that are pushing you into the arms of other women: Congratulations, you are a little Bitch.

If you make someone work harder than it should just because you know that person can go higher in their position than you: Congratulations, you are a little Bitch.

Simply put, men can be great Pentches. They work hard, work their asses off for what they have, and mind their own business. If you are respectful, care for people, get your shit done, take care of your kids, and help around the family, whether by working or home, I salute you. Join the hustler's club.

We love you. We get it.

And just like great Bitches, pentches can also find themselves stuck inside a dumbfuckery. All it takes is an acknowledgment that they're there to step out.
A guy hurting someone by disrespecting their partner can open their eyes and see. A guy missing from their kid's life

can pick up a phone and call. A guy being a dick at work, purposely hurting someone's chances of a career, can step back.

Just like us, they can step out of the dumbfuckery and join the wonderland.

Chapter 8: Dealing with Mean Bitches

The first thing to know is that once you defend yourself and slap someone with some Bitch-Dom, you will let it go and leave it. Sometimes, people escalate issues, and that's just a one-way ticket to some ass-kicking and straight into another Dumbfuckery.

Slapping someone with Bitch-Dom is as easy as putting up your hand to their face and saying, "Leave me the fuck alone," It is as easy as blocking people's numbers. It is as easy as cutting hurtful people out. Poof! Begone! That's it. Cut these bitches off. If you live with the bitches, you have the right to walk away, close the door and put a stop to it. No one should force you to anything.

Set boundaries. Say STOP.

Remember, we don't change people. People change themselves or mature over time, but we do not have the power to change others.

Now, if you have someone who still bugs, even after telling them to stop. Gather some word ammunition and reign on their asses. Forcefully tell them you do not want them near and shut the door. Assuming they are not physically hurtful or threatening, shut every communication off right away. If they are hurtful, seek professional help.

When a mean Bitch is present, the great thing to do is leave if you can. Once the Dumb Bitch realizes you can defend yourself, they usually walk away and leave you alone. Shrug your shoulders and walk. Bully release. Telling someone to mind their business usually works. The Bitches will understand that this is a boundary you do not want crossed, and they usually stop when they realize they have no power over you.

If they keep it up, then subtle comebacks are usually the best. I have a friend whose ex-boyfriend was a douchebag. He would take advantage of her, make her spend money, and even suggest she get a 9-5 since he didn't believe her baking business would take off. Mind you; his stupid ass got his car repossessed, never really respected her, and didn't have a stable job himself.

He constantly criticized her. He kept telling her she would never get herself a decent car and always complained about her old car because it would break down, and according to him: it was shameful for people to see them trying to fix it outside his house.

My friend, let's call her Mary, said that she saw him one day at a bus stop. "I wanted him to see me inside my new car, and for a moment, I wanted to give him a ride so that he could see how I was doing." She said.

After a year without him, her weekends are filled with baking orders. She went from having no bank account to paying her bills, buying herself a new car, and now looking for a new place to live. Her Bitch-dom took over quite nicely.

Was it going to feel great to show Douchebag that she made it? Was it going to feel great showing and proving him wrong? Was it going to feel great asking if he needed a ride inside her new car?

Yes. Yes. And yes.

But, remember, we need to let little Bitches go. Her greatest satisfaction came from seeing where he was and where she was standing in her life. His words meant nothing. She continued. She persevered even when facing many Mean-Bitches, telling her otherwise. She drove by, smiled, and continued. Bitch-dom right there.

If he kept persisting; if he kept bugging her about it even after breaking up (yes, there are people like that), she could have peeled right in front of him, dropped off a few dollars, and I would have encouraged her to yell, "Here asshole, let me pay your monthly bus fee, Bitch!" while driving off like a badass. But she didn't.

Another friend, Betty, has always been criticized by her family for not following in her parent's footsteps. They believe she is fucking up her life and that studying graphic design is a waste of time. When family comes over, she overhears her dad talking shit, and she has always been compared to her siblings. She works making logos for people, works for a company as a website marketing director, and has a side business that brings in extra cash for monthly endeavors.

Her parents? No.
She never brings it up.
She never speaks of money. She simply comes home and into her room. She does pay rent, pays bills, and pays for her car. Her parents know nothing. Her satisfaction is subtle. They do not need to know that great things are happening now or how much she is making. She simply pays her dues and continues.

Another friend: Let's call this one Darla. Darla cooks. Her parents insist she quits and finds herself a job where she will be unhappy. Her dad has gone as far as shutting off the gas in the kitchen because he wants to pressure her to quit her dream, which, in my opinion, is truly a fucked-up move. After an event, Darla made about a grand.

She knows not all events will do the same, but she prepares for both good and bad. For example, she told me she paid her dad cash for something she owed him, and he was dumbstruck.

Her satisfaction was the shut-the-fuck-up-ness of her parents. Yes, even parents can be Bitches sometimes. This wasn't a subtle move because she needed to escalate flashing her cash since they have been Bitching about her job for months. She tried to keep her money income a secret, but her parents kept insisting.

Every situation is different, and you have to differentiate what situation will work best with you.

Usually, when someone is a Bitch, two things are happening:

One: They are in fear of what you're doing. Sometimes, people get internally jealous of you and assume everything you're doing is wrong and stupid. Here is where you have friends and family trying to show you that they're better when they aren't. They simply could not put themselves in your shoes because your shoes are terrifying.

Or Two: The Bitch feels entitled to control you. Even strangers have this sickness. Especially family and friends, even parents. After all, if our parents could buy a house and provide shelter and food for six kids, they know something we don't, right? *Wrong.*

Remember that back in the day, things were more affordable. Houses were not super expensive. There were not tons of people in a type of career, things were just less inflated, and college didn't amount to fucking hundreds of thousands of dollars worth of payments and interests.

But we can't get angry with our parents. They just want the best for us. They do not want us to struggle the way they did, so when you do something that scares them, they can't vocalize it. But it's OK. Remember, every head is a world, and every path is different. So follow your dreams and improve yourself.

Work for yourself, never for others.

Sometimes, when people criticize (especially family members), it is a form of misguided caring. Simply because they don't know what is REALLY going on, and they "worry" without questioning or asking what the situation is. Now, for you: The only thing you have in your power is to let it go. (*Cue Frozen's Let it Go song.*) Understand that maybe they can't vocalize their "worry" using proper words or respect. And in the end, again, that is NOT YOUR Problem. It is theirs.

If you are close to family members, share your goals and dreams. If you are not, then it's cool, too. Your family will begin to understand that what you're doing is for your own life. Not theirs. They have done their part for their own life. It is time to make yours happen, no matter what decisions you make.

Relatives make the mistake of always using "I have been there, you need to learn from me," but the truth is, no one will learn from anyone unless they fall within the same stone themselves. As a mother, I hate understanding that, but I do. I have to.

If your family doesn't understand your decisions, then there is nothing you can do. They simply don't have the mentality to be open-minded about your choices, and we have to ignore the comments.

And this is where I find myself being called "The Black Sheep," "The One-That-Never-Listens," "The Corajuda" (Loosely Translated to The Angry Bitch)

Besides, "The Black Sheep" has such bullshit meaning because black sheep means to them that I talk only when I am pissed. Black sheep implies that I rebel against their belief system and don't follow through with their wonderful Mexican you-leave-the-house-when-you're-married tradition. Black Sheep "give parents headaches; they tend to argue often and fight with people."

This is a bullshit definition if you ask me.

To me, Black Sheep don't believe in being a kiss ass to everyone. We fight for our emotional freedom and try to be at peace with ourselves. We fight against traditional thinking, and because we do that, we are the "bad ones."

I personally like Black Sheep. For it is those artists that thrive. I have seen Black Sheep become great CEOs. Another start their own business. I have seen one create one of the biggest brands we use now, some have written the best novels, and some have become excellent teachers.

So there you go. Let them call you a black sheep. You'll thank them later.

As for the family-Bitches, you might have to understand that parents and family usually have issues beyond yourself, and honestly, out of your reach. People tend to never deal with the problems that they direct it to someone they love. This happens with everyone, especially with older generations.

And it's their issue.

I wouldn't suggest lifting a middle finger to family and friends unless they hurt you.

When it comes to family and friends, the best way to be a Bitch is to state the truth when it comes to you. Say what is bothering you and let it go. Most of them will not handle it, but that isn't your problem. Stating what bothers you is the key to making yourself a great Bitch.

Again, once you say it, you leave it. Let it go. Walk away proud that you voiced what you thought and never held it in. With respect, you raised a metaphorical baroque-Esque middle finger to their faces. Now, time for some badass tea.

Most self-help books will advise on just proving people wrong. If your parents complain about the boyfriend you have or the job you chose to take, people say, "Prove them wrong, and they'll see,"

"Show them you can."

Again, we live in an Instagram world where we need to show people everything we do. I advise staying away from that.

If you see my Instagram, I post where my business stuff is. I post when I go out and memes (lots of memes), but you never see my personal life. The life is hidden in between the sheets, my dates, my times at home, my own time.

I treasure privacy in an un-private world.

I treat people the same way.

You don't need to prove anyone wrong. You don't need to show them how much you make. You don't need to show them how good your boyfriend treats you. You don't even need to show them what kind of decisions you're making.

Wait. Let me step back a bit.

When you pay your bills, when you pay your car, when you pay rent, you don't need to show anyone anything.

Why do you think we are riddled with anxiety and social stress? Because we feel the need to report to people and always be present for everyone.
No. No. No!

If you rather sit at home watching TV than going out. Fine. If you choose to stop selling purses and begin selling couches. Fine. It is your life. No excuses!

Remember when I said if you have a partner, a romantic partner, that this doesn't apply? Don't be a dumbass and start spending the money your husband or wife gave you just because I said DO IT. No.
You chose to be with someone and join heads. You both work towards a goal, and you have fought hard to do so.

Maybe a small, "Hey babe, I'm going to buy one thousand dollars worth of beauty supplies" might suffice. Though, I think he will drop his jaw and demand a little chit-chat just then.

In actuality, remember this, you control your own life. You can choose to be a mean Bitch, a little Bitch, or a Dumb Bitch, but remember, that doesn't make you happy. My ticket way to Bitch-dom is to make you happy with yourself.

So speak up, Bitch.

Chapter 9: The Humble Bitch

Staying humble is one of the biggest lessons I have learned throughout my life. I have helped many people. I love remembering where I came from and where I struggled the most. I know that if I ever become a millionaire and if the Academy Awards finally offers me a nomination, I will raise my Oscar and remember I once had to sell my stuff just to get gas.

I also realized that people's definition of Staying Humble means Being-A-Broke-Bitch. Staying humble doesn't mean that in any way. You cannot feed the poor when you cannot feed yourself first. Not to mention giving your money away when you are not where you feel comfortable.

At one time, I decided to put on a charity event. I wanted to be able to gather money for children. I had the charity all picked up, and I asked people about location pricing and hours in which my event would go on. I had spent many hours planning children's activities, shows, live bands to benefit the event, and donation amounts.

Then I realized I have nothing myself to fall into. I was late on bills, I had bills on collections, and I was getting myself situated with being a newly single mother. I wanted to show gratitude that I could finally provide for my kid, and I felt like wanting to help others. A universal thank you, if you may.

My decision was an excellent one.

Fuck, I was doing shit for others.

It was awesome! (Nobel Prize shit)

When a friend who was helping me with this event said: "Yes, this is a wonderful idea, but make sure you are good yourself first." It made so much sense since I was putting in a lot of money from my pocket to the event, and I couldn't provide entirely for myself just yet.

This was when a spark plug happened again inside my anus. No. I wasn't a dumb Bitch because I was helping others. I was planning such goodness that this didn't qualify me as a dumb Bitch. I was just focusing my priorities on the wrong things. I had to focus on fixing my credit and getting myself a new car since my old one was having issues. Then, I had to focus on getting my bills paid off, getting shit done on my own. I needed to put myself first.

Staying humble means, yes, helps others, but fucking take care of yourself first. We feel we owe people everything, but fuck, you owe nothing to anyone (unless you asked for money and you need to pay that back.) Take care of your shit and then help others. Do it right.

Staying humble also means don't be an Entitled Bitch. People do not owe you anything, and life isn't revolving around you. If you have a great car, a huge house, and seventy-seven Louis Vuitton bags, that's awesome! But, it doesn't make you better than anyone or vice versa. Remember, at one point, you had nothing.

When I purchased my new car, a tiny Nissan Versa, I had some people scoff and mutter under their breath, "Why didn't you get a better one?" I was surrounded by people who believe that having a Corvette meant you were wealthy, and those appearances were everything. I was driving my car in embarrassment because I was paying 175 dollars instead of paying 400 dollars like I "should have." And not until I began to cut these people

off, I drove my car with pride because

FUCK! IT'S A NEW CAR!!

Appearances are nothing. Money, in the end, is nothing.

When you have 100,000,000 in the bank, and I have 100,

we sleep the same way. We sit down on the toilet to take a

shit the same way, our farts smell the same, and we brush

our teeth the same way.

Staying humble means don't flaunt the appearance of being

rich. It also means you don't give away your survival

assets.

Just be a Humble Bitch.

Chapter 10: Be a Humorous Bitch

Another short chapter. I will not dwell too much on it because it is very self-explanatory.

Have a sense of humor.

Be able to laugh at yourself, at life's situations, and everyday occurrences. Don't walk around with a super stick up your ass.

We live in an overly offended world that anything said is used against us. It sucks. People have been fired over postings on Facebook and Instagram. Everyone has something to say, and everyone has something to be offended about. We cannot say a word without someone batting their eyes, holding their chest, and inhaling such "offensive comments."

Comedians aren't even safe anymore. We are all walking (no, fucking cross-country running) into a politically correct world, and I disagree.

Sure, some things are overboard. Some things should not be said sometimes, but every situation is different. Everyone should use common sense to find out where and what can be said.

We can't say "Happy Halloween!" without offending certain religions. We can't say, "Bring Home the Bacon!" anymore without having a tsunami of Vegans on our backs. We can't even say, "You Go Girl!" without being slapped in the face.

And don't get me started with not allowing our children to lose tournaments and championships. Who the fuck benefits from "We are all winners!" Sporting events?!

"Uh... Excuse me... Who Da Fuck Won? I got some bets to pay off!"

I want to say, "Merry Christmas!"

I want to say, "Fuck yeah, I'm hysterical!"

I want to say, "Check your blind spot!"

Sue me. *(Please don't)*

If a comedian talks about fat people, I laugh. I laugh my ass off. It's true! And if I love to eat like a fat-fuck, I do it too! So stop being horrendously offended over everything.

Now, off to In-N-Out for a Double-Double.

Chapter 11: It Works, Bitch!

I talked a lot about things.

-Keeping it real

-Being realistic with yourself.

-Speaking the truth

-Being respectful

-Staying humble

But why does it all work? Why does being a great Bitch work? Remember, this is all for you.

I'm not saying you have to become fucking Hulk and Hulk-smash everyone that crosses your path. I'm saying be delicate with yourself, accept your beauties and your flaws the way they are, and the way they're evolving.

My goal isn't to make you feel uncomfortable, but speaking the truth will make you feel that way. Why hold it in? For what purpose? To save someone else's feelings? Is that worth it?

I know there will be situations where holding in some feelings will benefit you more than letting them out, but I trust you to choose which moments will work for you and which will not. Sometimes, things are better left unsaid. However, don't keep everything inside. Looking within and letting that hurt come out will help you heal.

People don't like me speaking the truth. Sometimes, it isn't so pretty. I am sarcastic and joke around. On the other spectrum, I am insightful, and I care for people. I want them to be happy. I want to see someone feeling hopeful and motivated because I was once stuck. I, too, have only stared at the dark. And I don't want anyone to feel like suffocating.

The world is ugly through saddened eyes. And I have also felt like there was no way out. But there is.

I state what I believe when I believe it. And every time I do, I feel better. That's just how it works—knowing what things to say and when to speak up is a great feeling. This happens when you study your past and work within yourself.

And once you realize you have reached Bitch-dom, your body relaxes: Your shoulders drop, your face becomes calm, you simply allow comments, insults, and attitudes to roll off. If you don't, you figure out how: writing, working, swimming, cutting people off, throat-punching. (Totally kidding on the throat-punching)

As for me, when I began Bitch-up, I slept better. For someone who had insomnia, I struggled to get a full four hours of sleep. I had back pain, body pain, headaches, and my patience would be lost in seconds. I still lose my patience but not emotionally. I'm just an impatient bitch. And I'm working on that.

After entering Bitch-Dom, I felt great. It was a massive weight off my shoulders. I could breathe correctly, and my nails weren't in danger of being bitten off to their core. Now, I look forward to work. I look forward to a challenge. Even traffic doesn't bother me. I enjoy my drive to work and home (Well, sometimes.... because I am still considering writing *The Art of Not Driving Like A Fucking Dumbass!)* I enjoy dinner and lunches with family, going to karaoke bars, meeting people, spending time with my son, and even going to pay bills feels satisfying.

Why?

Because I let my Inner-Bitch talk when she feels it. And I do it respectfully. I don't scream. I am not a Karen or go crazy. I am poised, calm, and follow the rules.

I don't hate the world (I once did).

I don't hate everyone (I once did too).

Sure, there will be days when I feel I won't get through it, but I have faith that it will get better. I also understand that my depression will come back, and I will have to visit those demons inside my head. I know I will wake up feeling lonely or sad again. I know that.

It is there where I will decide to deal with it in my way (without hurt); life throws many curveballs, and well, sometimes they knock us down.

In October 2018, I saw my son's unconscious body on my kitchen floor after an asthma attack. I had no paramedics near, and my dad ran out to yell for help. As I saw his purple lips, I thought I was going to become a mourning mother. A mother without a child. At that moment, everything I had gone through meant nothing. This was the worst.

Thank all the Gods and all the heavens that I didn't. Being in the hospital for two weeks, I began to panic. My world was shaken. I never wanted to leave. I wanted doctors by my side 24/7. I wanted to ask the hospital how much rent was so I could move in. I was terrified of being home because the home was traumatizing.

As we walked inside the entry door and back home, I slept with one eye open. My drive to work and back was daunting. I was reliving the moment in my head for weeks. But I had to calm down. I had to walk in and speak nicely to my inner demons, hoping one of them would listen. And within, someone did speak.

One demon turned into an angel in disguise. He walked me through the trauma. We let those feelings of fear and panic out into the open. And I could breathe a little again. As hurtful as that moment was for me, I know things will be better. Situations will get better, and we will find solutions. Of course, I was lucky. But, sadly, sometimes, people aren't so. And that is just heartbreaking.

The Art of Being a Bitch is moving onto the next day: being prepared, taking action, making changes, and stepping onto the next thing.

I am CPR certified, numbers for emergency departments are on speed dial, we have an emergency box with items to use in case, and we visit the doctors often.

Some people are too afraid to make a change.

But don't worry. It is going to be OK.

Make the change.

For years, people (not just women) have been stepping back and letting the other person take a position, the cake, the last piece of pizza. I'm not saying have a galaxial battle for a slice of pepperoni pizza either; I'm just saying that if the opportunity is there, make yourself happy first. Talk about it, make plans and respectfully take the challenge. You deserve it. We all do.

Be aware that I am not saying copy anyone's life. Do not go off and steal people's ideas. I am not saying screw up your friends by doing what they do and taking their treasure. A badass Bitch will find her market and strike at the right opportunity.

126

Care for yourself and care for the people you love and who are dear to your heart. Care for those that you want in your life for years to come. Don't worry about Ana, or average Joe, if you do not see them in your life in the next ten years. I care for a lot of people.

I do.

I'm not a heartless Bitch. I just care for those that I see in my future. Don't feel sorry for having feelings. Don't feel ashamed because you want good things for yourself, and don't be sorry when you hit a golden opportunity and someone else hasn't. Trust me; their golden opportunity is gonna come too. It isn't your concern.

The Good Bitch, the Bad Bitch, the Badass Bitch, cares for the world while taking care of herself. The great Bitch makes shit happen without screwing people over. The badass Bitch manages and cares for herself. The good Bitch does not stress to control others.

Yes. I find myself in a Dumbfuckery right now.

You see, I have a bit of OCD. (I can hear my friends yelling, "A BIT??") Whenever I find myself at an art show, and the person next to me is messy, has shit loads of trash, and doesn't worry about trip hazards, my eye twitches.

BUT...

As a Good Bitch, I remain silent. That is when I let it go because I have to.

If I were a mean Bitch, I would go and complain to the city's Health Department. I will walk up into their space, perform an accident to sue them, and teach them a lesson (exaggerating, of course,) but I ignore it. If it isn't within my 10 feet of rented space, I worry not.

I can't.

I am far too busy working on my shit that if they want a lawsuit, fine, let them.

But I am honest. If someone mentions it, I often voice it. Just ask my friend Liz...

I often joke around with friends, too. I say things that are a little overboard. If you had a microphone in my car, I would be burnt at the stake. (Don't get any ideas,) But we are kidding. I have a crude sense of humor, so a lot of people don't get it, and that's OK.

Humor is my coping mechanism.

But when I am asked for advice, I am as honest as I can be. Sometimes, I might be wrong, but at that moment, I think it's true. I am trying to help. Unless you just want to vent, and then I just turn into a hugging pillow.

At one point in my life, I was told I was a liar, and that hurt more than when I fell down a snowy mountain, cracking all my bones and gasping for air while my mom was laughing. It was there when I said, "fuck it, you beautiful Bitch, let slap you with some truth," and then I snapped out of it.

I rushed out of that dumbfuckery right away because, for years, I had been trying to sugar coat things for people, and they ended up coming back to me, making the same mistakes. I try to be the Best Bitch I can for you, and I always will.

If you are willing to try the exercises in this book and speak the truth, you'll find your own level of Bitch-dom.
And to let you know: My Bitch-dom will not match yours.
But we will share the same post office.

So I raise a glass to you.

Because being a Badass Bitch is an art. Art that some people might not understand. You will have some people staring at this book like a contemporary abstract art piece in the middle of an art gallery. Their hands will rest under their chin, and they will contemplate the weird shit I have talked to you about today.

Some people will get it. Some people will be too scared. Some people will take it too far and get sucker punched. (I warned you. It hurts.) And others will make a change for the worst: closing their minds even further (but worry not, we are evolving creatures, and change will happen at their time)

As for most of us, we will understand the power of being true to ourselves. The beauty of putting your ass on a pedestal and wearing your crown without running people over. Because fuck, it feels great!

I hope you understood my language, quotes, dumb Bitch stories, and roads through Dumbfuckery. I hope to see you inside the great Bitch-dom of life. Unless you catch me inside a dumbfuckery, which in that case, I'd invite you for a quick drink and drive out because, well, life goes both ways, and we know this will be a normal stepping stool into Bitch-dom.

I am sure I will never be entirely perfectly settled inside Bitch-dom. It doesn't happen that way. I will fall, cause havoc inside my brain, trip and fall into broke-hood, stress-hood, dumb Bitch-hood many times.

We all will.

That's the beauty of life.

We get to experience the downs and ups on this roller coaster. Enjoy every moment because life is short. Life is just a stairway to heaven's way into the highway of hell and back.

A perfect circle of life.

Now, let's get through this bridge of heavens and hells we call life.

From a Badass Bitch to another, I salute you.

Social Media Link

Instagram.com/kcmendozabooks

#theartofbeingabitch

Email Me Your Inner Badass Stories

kcmendozabooks@gmail.com

Helpful Links

www.mentalhealth.gov

www.samhsa.gov (Substance Abuse and Mental Health Services)

www.nami.org (Natural Alliance on Mental Illness)

Photography/Cover Photo

A special thanks to my cousin Jose Roberto Arellano for photo shooting my egotistical ass for the front cover photo.

www.facebook.com/robertoarellanojrfotografia